NATIVE AMERI DESIGNS

COLORING BOOK

Marty Noble

DOVER PUBLICATIONS
GARDEN CITY, NEW YORK

You'll delight in the variety of images in this coloring tribute to the beauty and symbolism of Native American designs. Crafts such as the popular dreamcatcher as well as pottery and basketwork display beautifully symmetrical motifs. Also included are Kokopelli, the flute player; intricately carved totems; and Native American clothing and masks—all enclosed in wonderfully imaginative decorative borders. Just select your media and experiment with the colors of your choice as you enjoy the artistic possibilities of this unique collection—plus, the perforated, unbacked pages make displaying your work easy!

Bibliographical Note

Native American Designs Coloring Book is a new work, first published by Dover Publications in 2017.

International Standard Book Number

ISBN-13: 978-0-486-81745-3
ISBN-10: 0-486-81745-8

Manufactured in the United States by LSC Communications Book LLC
81745808   2021
www.doverpublications.com